LAUREATE OF PESSIMISM

THE
LAUREATE of PESSIMISM

A SKETCH OF THE LIFE
AND CHARACTER OF

JAMES THOMSON ("B.V.")

Author of "THE CITY OF DREADFUL NIGHT."

BY
BERTRAM DOBELL

KENNIKAT PRESS
Port Washington, N. Y./London

THE LAUREATE OF PESSIMISM

First published in 1910
Reissued in 1970 by Kennikat Press
Library of Congress Catalog Card No: 77-105781
ISBN 0-8046-1013-4

Manufactured by Taylor Publishing Company   Dallas, Texas

PREFATORY NOTE.

⟐

WHEN in 1884 I edited the posthumous volume of
Thomson's works, entitled "A Voice from the Nile,
and other Poems," I prefixed to it a brief memoir of
the author. This memoir, revised and enlarged, was
also prefixed to the complete edition of Thomson's
"Poetical Works," published in 1895. It has always
been my desire to write a full biography of the poet,
which should include as complete a collection of his
letters as can now be made. Many hindrances have
prevented me, up to the present time, from carrying
out my design; and at the age at which I have now
arrived I must not too confidently rely upon my
ability to accomplish it. Meanwhile, as Mr. Salt's
excellent "Life of Thomson" is now out of print, it
seems desirable that some account of the poet, in an
inexpensive form, should be made available. That
must be my apology—if apology be needed—for the
publication of the present imperfect sketch. Of its
deficiencies no one can be more sensible than myself;
but it has seemed to me that in this case, as in so
many others, it is better that the thing should be done
imperfectly than not done at all.

The present sketch is founded on that which is prefixed to the complete edition of Thomson's poems.
Some passages, however, which will be found in the
original essay have been omitted; but, on the other
hand, a good many additions have been made to it.
Many matters which I should have liked to dwell
upon have perforce been passed over in the present

essay : but I hope that enough has been said to make the reader desire to acquaint himself more intimately, through the study of Thomson's writings, with the mental and moral nature of one of the finest and rarest spirits of the last century. The essay is, in short, published with the hope and expectation that it will increase considerably the number of Thomson's readers and admirers. Though he will, I suppose, never be a "popular poet"—which means no more, perhaps, than a poet whose works have an extensive sale, though it may be doubted if more than a few of those who buy them ever read them—his works, I think, should be known to a far larger number of readers and students than is now the case. If anyone chooses to say that, in this case, I am hardly an impartial judge, I shall not be particularly anxious to rebut the accusation. That I was of some use to the unfortunate poet in his lifetime is one of my most cherished memories ; and it is now, as it always has been, my earnest desire to keep alive and extend the fame of "B. V." by all the means within my power. I daresay there are many faults of omission and commission in the present sketch ; but if it fulfils the purpose which I have had in view in writing it, I shall not complain of any severity of censure that may be bestowed upon its shortcomings.

THE LAUREATE OF PESSIMISM

A S Thomson is one of the commonest of names
and James seems to sort peculiarly well with
it, it is no wonder that a good many James
Thomsons are recorded in bibliographies as having
written plays, poems, and other works ; but of these
it is safe to say that two only are likely to be
remembered in the future, namely, the authors of
"The Seasons" and "The City of Dreadful Night."
Excepting the name, the two poets had perhaps as
little in common as any two poets ever had. The
first James Thomson seems to have been in most
respects about as fortunate as it was possible for
him to be : the second could not well have been
more unfortunate than he was. Yet, save for the
inherited defects and peculiarities of his temperament, there was perhaps no reason why the latter
poet should not have had as prosperous a career as
his predecessor. He was—at any rate in my
opinion—far superior in genius and in general
mental power to the author of "The Seasons" ;
but while the one was able to make the utmost of
such talents as he possessed, because they were
such as appealed to the widest circle of readers, the
other had few or no gifts which could recommend
him to the uncultured or uncritical crowd. Since
even Matthew Arnold—who, in Thomson's place,
might very well have written "The City of Dreadful

Night," while Thomson, brought up as Arnold was,
might conceivably have been the author of "Literature and Dogma"—was unable to make a sufficient
income by his pen to supply his wants, it is no
wonder that "B.V.," suffering under the dis-
advantages of poverty and unpopular opinions, was
scarcely able to gain a bare subsistence by his
writings, and remained almost to the end of his
career unknown and unappreciated.   He dared to
transgress that most stringent of all the command-
ments of the British Philistine, " Thou shalt, before
all else, be respectable," and he paid the due penalty
for his contumacy.

James Thomson was born at Port Glasgow on
November 23, 1834.   He was thus a scion of the
Victorian period, and though he was during his
whole life at war with most of its tendencies, it was
not the less impossible for him to escape from being
influenced by the spirit of the time.   Even the
revolter against convention, however he may strive
against its influence, cannot altogether eliminate
its virus from his veins.   Had Thomson been born
a generation later he would, I think, have had a
happier life, and would have found a much more
sympathetic and appreciative audience.

The poet's father was a sailor in the merchant
service, in which he attained a good position and
prospered well, until, in 1840, when, acting as chief
officer of the ship *Eliza Stewart*, of Greenock, he
was disabled by a paralytic stroke, the result, it is
said, of a week of terrible storm, during which
he was unable to change his drenched clothing.
Up to this time he had been of a cheerful disposition, and a delightful companion; but now
a change for the worse took place, and his temper
became strange, moody, and uncertain.   He lived

on till 1853, but in a state of weakness of mind which prevented him from providing for his sons, or from acting as a wise guardian towards them. The poet's mother was a deeply religious woman, and a devoted follower of Edward Irving. She was of a highly emotional and imaginative temperament, and it was from her, no doubt, that her son inherited the deep vein of melancholy in his disposition. It was a great misfortune for him that she died when he was little more than eight years old.

In December, 1842, James Thomson was admitted to that excellent institution, the Royal Caledonian Asylum, through the kind exertions of some friends of his parents. There he remained for the next eight years. This was probably the happiest period of his life. His lessons were mastered quickly and easily ; he got on well with his schoolfellows ; and he took his due share in all the sports and pastimes that were going on. Pessimism indeed rarely afflicts the young ; they are far too busily occupied in living for "the bitter, old, and wrinkled truth" of the hollowness and hopelessness of human life to reveal itself to them. Thomson's teachers and fellow-pupils saw nothing uncommon in him, excepting that he was much above the average in mental capacity.

Thomson quitted the Asylum in 1850 to become a monitor in the "Model School" at the Royal Military College, Chelsea. It had been decided that his future profession should be that of an army-schoolmaster, and it was necessary to qualify for this post at the above-named college. This was hardly the profession which Thomson would have adopted had he been free to choose for himself ; but it was the only one which would put him at once in the way of gaining a living, because any other would have entailed a period of probation during which he would have had no means of existence.

After having gone through the prescribed course of study at the college, Thomson left it in order to take up the post of assistant-teacher in the garrison-school at Ballincollig, a village near Cork. This was in pursuance of the usual course, which required that candidates for the post of army-schoolmaster should act for a time in a subordinate capacity before being appointed. Thomson's duty at Ballincollig was to teach in the regimental school under the direction of Joseph Barnes, the garrison-master. He became an inmate of the household of Mr. and Mrs. Barnes, by both of whom he was much beloved, and who treated him with the utmost kindness. With them he was for a brief period entirely happy, or at least as much so as it was possible for him to be. In a series of sonnets, written some ten or twelve years later, the poet recalls

> The tender memories, the moonlight dreams,
>   Which make your home an ever-sacred shrine,
> And show your features lit with heavenly gleams.

It was in the home of these ever-dear and ever tenderly remembered friends that he first met his "Good Angel," the young girl who might, if she had lived, have saved him from becoming an inhabitant of that "City of Dreadful Night" in whose sombre shades he was destined to wander for so many mournful and joyless years, though he was destined to find there the material most fit for his genius to exert itself upon, and the inspiration which he needed to spur him to the accomplishment of his greatest work. I only say her influence

might have saved him from his life-long melancholia, because the constitutional causes from which
it sprang were perhaps too deeply rooted to be
overcome even by the most favourable outward
circumstances. Nevertheless, it seems likely that
if she had lived he might so far have overcome the
fits of gloom and life-weariness from which he
suffered as to be afflicted by them only at intervals,
and then not to an intolerable degree. So at any
rate he thought himself :—

" You would have kept me from the burning sands
     Bestrewn with bleaching bones,
  And led me through the friendly fertile lands,
     And changed my weary moans
  To hymns of triumph and enraptured love,
  And made our earth as rich as heaven above."

This young girl was the daughter of the armourer-
sergeant of a regiment which was then quartered at
Ballincollig. Her name was Matilda Weller, and
she was then about fourteen years of age. That
she was an attractive and beautiful creature seems
certain, however much the young poet's imagination
may have idealised or transfigured her.

At this time Thomson had not yet reached his
eighteenth year, and therefore, it may be thought,
was hardly old enough to conceive a serious and
lasting love-passion. It is true that such cases of
youthful affection are common, and that they
seldom outlast the period of boyhood and girlhood ;
but Thomson at eighteen was more advanced in all
manly qualities than most young men who have
reached their majority : and, as must needs be the
case with all true poets, there was in him an un-
usually early awakening of the passion of love. It
is certain that Thomson's affection for Matilda
Weller was no mere passing fancy, but was a deep

and abiding passion which affected his whole life, upon which it had a greater influence than any other event which happened to him.

It was at Ballincollig also that he first became acquainted with Charles Bradlaugh, who was then a private soldier in a dragoon regiment which was stationed in the village. Of the friendship which was formed between the two young men much might be said were space available : here it can only be noted that in spite of their very different characters they at once became fast friends and comrades, and remained so, not, unfortunately, to the end, but for upwards of twenty eventful years.

After remaining at Ballincollig for rather more than seventeen months, Thomson returned to the "Normal School," Chelsea, in order to complete the course of studies which it was necessary to go through before being finally appointed to the post of army-schoolmaster. At this time all things were apparently going well with him, and a career, not brilliant it might be, but yet somewhat better than the common lot, seemed to be in store for him. He had already resolved to gain distinction as a poet, and meanwhile his position in the army would secure him from that soul-destroying struggle for the mere means of subsistence. which has exhausted the energies and destroyed the powers of so many aspiring and finely-gifted spirits. But soon the blow fell upon him which was to destroy all his hopes of happiness. One morning in July, 1853, he received a letter containing the news that Miss Weller was dangerously ill : the next morning he heard that she was dead. That this was an overwhelming blow to him, and that it affected his whole after-life, can hardly be doubted. All his hopes and all his plans for the future had been bound up with her; and with her death his chief aim in life had been destroyed. Henceforth his existence was that of one whose will was broken, and who cared not whither he wandered, since there was nowhere a Mecca or a Promised Land wherein he might hope to find rest and peace. It has indeed been doubted whether this event did really affect him so deeply, and it has been argued that it was rather the *occasion* than the *cause* of his life-long unhappiness. Some other cause or causes, it has been urged, would have produced the same result even if Miss Weller had lived. As Carlyle said, with regard to Novalis, whose case was somewhat similar to Thomson's—

"That the whole philosophical and moral existence of such a man should have been shaped and determined by the death of a young girl, almost a child, specially distinguished, so far as is shown, by nothing save her beauty,* which at any rate must have been very short-lived, will doubtless seem to everyone a singular concatenation. We cannot but think that some result precisely similar in moral effect might have been attained by many different means; nay, that by one means or another it would not have failed to be attained."

Whether it does or does not indicate an excessive weakness of character to be so profoundly affected by the death of a beloved one I will not now stop to consider. What is certain is that such cases of deep and abiding sorrow for loved and lost ones are by no means uncommon among ordinary mortals who have no claim to the possession of

---

* " By nothing save her beauty ! " Surely a very unhappy remark : as if one should say of Hercules that he was distinguished by nothing save his strength ; or of Shakespeare that his only gift was his imagination !

genius. It surely argued a certain insensibility of feeling on Carlyle's part to reason from his own consciousness that *he* would not have been so influenced by a young girl's death, that therefore Novalis, whose character differed altogether from his, could not have been so affected !

Whether, even if Miss Weller had lived, Thomson would not still have suffered from his constitutional unhappiness, it is surely vain to enquire, since it must at best be a matter of mere conjecture. "What's done we partly may compute," but not what might have happened if events had taken a different turn. I am myself unable to conceive of any other misfortune which would have affected Thomson as he was affected by the death of Miss Weller. For any other calamity he would, I believe, have found "some drop of comfort" in his soul, and would have endured it stoically enough. Let anyone who doubts the reality of Thomson's life-long sorrow and regret for his lost love read through his works, noting the many passages in which she is referred to, and doubt will then, I believe, be no longer possible.

In "A Lady of Sorrow," Thomson has described the successive phases through which his sorrow for his lost love passed. After recovering from the first stunning blow, Sorrow visited him as an Angel, or (partly at least) as an influence for good : then as a Siren, destroying for him all human delights, making him an alien from his kind, and afflicting him with distaste for "all the uses of the world" : and finally as a Shadow, ever present with him, ever weighing upon his spirits, ever driving him to muse upon the insoluble mysteries of life and death, and ever whispering that death is better than life, that life indeed is but a disease and a martyrdom, and that the grave only is man's true goal. This was the history of his inner life : outwardly he remained to his work-fellows and friends, after the first paroxysm of grief was over, much the same as he had been previously. Though he scarcely made a secret of the cause of his unhappiness, and most of his friends had an inkling of it, he does not seem to have taken any of them entirely into his confidence about it. Usually indeed he was very reticent as to his personal affairs, and only spoke about himself, or his literary work, when specially asked to do so.

Thomson finally enlisted as an army-school-master in August, 1854, his first appointment being to serve with a Militia regiment in Devonshire. Afterwards he joined the Rifle Brigade at Alder-shot, where he remained during 1855 and part of 1856. He was an efficient and painstaking teacher in spite of the fact that he had little or no liking for his chosen profession. He was always very methodical and exact in his ways, and his own thorough mastery of his subjects made it easy for him to impart his knowledge to his pupils. In a letter to a friend, written in familiar verse, he thus expressed his feelings with regard to his profession—

" — if now and then a curse (too intense for this light verse)
  Should be gathering in one's spirit when he thinks of how
    he lives,
  With a constant tug and strain, knowing well it's all in
    vain—
  Pumping muddy information into unretentive sieves,
  Let him stifle back the curse which but makes the matter
    worse,
  And by tugging on in silence earn his wages if he can ;
  For the blessèd eve and night are his own yet, and he
    might
  Fit sound bottoms to those sieves too were he not so weak
    a man."

From Aldershot Thomson was removed to Ireland in the summer of 1856, where he served with the 55th Foot, with which regiment he remained until he left the army. During the years 1856-60 he was stationed either at Dublin or the Curragh Camp. Here his life seems to have passed in a somewhat monotonous routine. He chafed against its dulness, and had a great longing for a more active and adventurous career. He even discussed with his friend, John Grant, who was, like himself, an army-schoolmaster, and at that time a great chum of his, a plan of deserting the army and going to sea. If he could have found an adequate field for the exercise and display of his practical abilities, the result would probably have been beneficial to him in the highest degree. But it would have been necessary that circumstances should force him into action ; for he was one of those in whom, as in Hamlet, the power of acting is enfeebled or destroyed by much brooding over the consequences of action. That he was quite conscious of this failing in himself is apparent from a poem which he wrote on his twenty-third birthday, wherein he reflects

> " With even less of grief than sharp self-scorn "

upon his wasted and misused early years, which should have brought strength, wisdom, faith and love, but have left him a prey to languor of spirit, unavailing regret, and disillusion.

> " All lost for ever ! and the hours to come,
>   Poor refuse ! but our sole remaining wealth,
> So much the likelier thence to share their doom !
>   The brain unused to mark insidious stealth,
> Short-sighted eyes long filled with mist and gloom,
>   Lax hands uncustomed to the grasp of health,
> That lost the fight in their best youth,—shall these
> Victorious prove in languor and disease ? "

It must be confessed that this poem shows the existence in its author of a somewhat morbid strain of mind, and of a spirit of self-accusation somewhat similar to that exhibited at religious revivals by the penitents who are anxious to show that they have been great sinners in the past in order to enhance the merit of their present state of grace. In Thomson it was probably the outcome of his mother's deep vein of piety; or rather perhaps a legacy derived from a long line of Calvinistic forefathers. It is certain that there was no real ground for the mood of penitence and self-reproach which this poem displays. At twenty-three it is far too early to despair, because one has not yet performed any great deeds or attained to a settled philosophy of life. That Thomson eventually got the better of this mood, and came at length to see that he was what he was by the law of his nature, and that by no conceivable means could he make himself otherwise, will be seen further on.

Unlike most poets, Thomson did not make a too-early appearance in print. It was in 1858, when he was twenty-four years of age, that his first verses were published. Much had been written before then, but he was wise enough in after-life to destroy the greater part of it. Therefore in his case there is no " Hours of Idleness," no " Wandering Jew," nor any other youthful folly to rise up in judgment against him. Those early poems of his which have been preserved—let us say roughly all those written before 1862, two or three only excepted—cannot be compared indeed for power, artistry, or concentration of thought with those written afterwards; but they are not to be dismissed as mere 'prentice work. They are all worth studying for their own sake, and not merely because they are the early effusions of a great writer. In all of them there is that "fundamental brainwork" which Dante Rossetti considered to be the most essential quality in any work of art. He was never content, as Browning often was, to leave his conceptions only half-realised, or imperfectly welded into shape, but always laboured upon them until he had clearly worked out his designs, and had used his best of art in putting them into form.

Thomson's first published poem appeared in February, 1858, in a small Freethought paper, entitled, the *London Investigator*. It was entitled "Mr. Save-his-Soul-Alive-O," and was signed "Bysshe Vanolis." This was the only occasion upon which he used the full signature : afterwards his poems and prose articles were signed "B. V." only. "Bysshe," it seems, was adopted out of his reverence for Shelley ; "Vanolis" appears to be an anagram of "Novalis," the pen-name of the German poet and mystic, Hardenberg, whose fate, like Thomson's, was largely influenced by the untimely death of a young girl to whom he was devotedly attached.

During 1858-1860 a good many of Thomson's early poems appeared in *Tait's Magazine*, over the signature of "Crepusculus." "Bertram to the Lady Geraldine," "Tasso to Leonora," "The Lord of the Castle of Indolence," and "A Festival of Life," were among the poems which he contributed to that periodical.

In 1858 Mr. Bradlaugh, who had left the army in the previous year, and was then fairly started on his career as a freethought writer and lecturer, became the editor of the before-mentioned periodical, the *London Investigator*. To this Thomson contributed essays on Burns and Emerson, and a prose allegory entitled "The King's Friends."

In June 1860, the regiment to which Thomson was attached was transferred from the Curragh Camp to Aldershot. This was a welcome change to Thomson, who had long been weary of his residence in Ireland. After his return to England he took the opportunity of renewing his friendship with some old friends of his parents and himself. These were Mr. and Mrs. Gray and their daughters. With one of the latter he had kept up a correspondence during his residence in Ireland. That lady (now Mrs. Greig) gives the following account of his visit to them at this time :—

"At last he wrote saying that he was to have a fortnight's holiday, and would pay us a visit. We were all excitement at his coming. I had previously informed him in one of my letters that Helen had become a Ragged School teacher, and in reply he had said he could not imagine a creature so bright, and, in his remembrance, so beautiful, being arrayed in sombre habiliments, and acting such a character. When he arrived Helen met him in the most demure manner possible, and kept up the delusion, or rather tried to do so, for he was not to be deceived. Two days after his arrival, when he was sitting reading, she suddenly sent something flying at his head, at which he started up, saying, 'Ah ! I have just been quietly waiting for this ! You have been acting a part which does not become you, but you have now resumed your true character, and are the Helen of old.' During this visit we thought him much altered in appearance and manners ; indeed we were somewhat disappointed. He was by no means so manly-looking as when he left London, and was painfully silent and depressed. He went from us with the intention of again going to

Aldershot, but from that day, until Mr. Maccall*
mentioned him to us, we never once heard of him.
Ever since, we have felt greatly puzzled to account for
his singular conduct."

It is no wonder that these young ladies, knowing
nothing of the story of his lost love, were unable to
account for his silence and depression. It is
strange, however, that he failed afterwards to keep
up his friendship with them. There is evidence to
show that he was neither ungrateful to them, nor
forgetful of their kindness; and the only probable
reason I can think of for his conduct, is that his
intense feeling of his supposed personal unworthi-
ness caused him to think himself unfitted to
associate with them. The passages I have quoted
from the poem on his twenty-third birthday have
shown how much he suffered from these moods of
self-reproach; and further evidence on the same
point is to be found in "Vane's Story," which is
really the poet's Autobiography and Apologia :—

> " I half remember, years ago,
> Fits of despair that maddened woe,
> Frantic remorse, intense self-scorn,
> And yearnings harder to be borne
> Of utter loneliness forlorn ;
> What passionate secret prayers I prayed !
> What futile firm resolves I made !
> As well a thorn might pray to be
> Transformed into an olive tree ;
> As well a weevil might determine
> To grow a farmer-hating vermin :
> The *I am that I am* of God
> Defines no less a worm or clod.

---

* William Maccall, author of "Elements of Individualism,"
and of many other remarkable but unappreciated works. He
published in 1886 a booklet entitled, "A Nirvana Trilogy :
three Essays on the Career and the Literary Labours of James
Thomson."

My penitence was honest guile ;
My inmost being all the while
Was laughing in a patient mood
At this externe solicitude,
Was waiting laughing till once more
I should be sane as heretofore ;
And in the pauses of the fits
That rent my heart and scared my wits,
Its pleasant mockery whispered through,
Oh, what can Saadi have to do
With penitence? and what can you?
Are Shiraz roses wreathed with rue? "

It will be noticed that the above passage, besides
recording the fits of despair "that rent my heart
and scared my wits," records also his deliverance
from them. The poem was written in 1864 ; and no
doubt he had at that time attained a calmer and
more stoical frame of mind. But I doubt if he ever
entirely vanquished these moods : for there are a
good many indications in his writings that show
that to the last he suffered bitterly from the feeling
that he was, in a sense, an outcast from humanity,
or one who had sinned almost too deeply to be
forgiven. Few poets can have been more dissimilar
in character and disposition than Cowper and
Thomson, yet there was a strange likeness between
them in the fact that each was afflicted with the
disease—for such it was in their cases—of self-
derogation or self-condemnation. Both were men
of acute sensibilities which verged upon, and sometimes overpassed, the borders of morbidity. Cowper's fits of insanity were paralleled by Thomson's
fits of intemperance. It was the same cause at
bottom which led Cowper to look upon himself as
a lost soul, and Thomson to regard the world as a
scene of black and immitigable despair. There
was in the latter poet, however, a kind of saner consciousness, which, though it did not save him from

suffering from the moods I have described, yet enabled him to see clearly, sometimes at least, the folly of them.   No one has satirised these desperate moods of self-derogation more keenly than Thomson has done in the following epigram :—

> " Once in a saintly passion
>   I cried with desperate grief,
> O Lord, my heart is black with guile,
>   Of sinners I am chief.
> Then stooped my guardian angel,
>   And whispered from behind,
> ' Vanity, my little man,
>   You're nothing of the kind.' "

In 1860 the *National Reformer* was established as an organ of the Freethought party, under the joint editorship of Joseph Barker and Charles Bradlaugh.   Dissensions, however, broke out between the two chiefs, and the paper soon presented the strange and amusing spectacle of a duello proceeding in its pages between its editors.   This could not last ; and eventually Barker, who, though now forgotten, was in his time a very able and popular journalist and lecturer, though he was a man of most unstable opinions, was ousted, and Bradlaugh became sole editor and proprietor of the *Reformer*, which he thenceforth controlled to the time of his death.   As was to be expected, Bradlaugh invited Thomson, with whom he had kept up a close correspondence since he had left the army, to contribute to his paper.   Thomson agreed to do so ; but his contributions were only occasional in the early years of the *Reformer's* existence.   His first important article in it was an essay on Shelley.   Another early contribution was his poem, entitled, " The Dead Year," which appeared in the number for January 6, 1861.   This is a fine but gloomy and pessimistic review, not so

much of the year 1860 as of the general course of
human affairs, which, in the eyes of the poet,
exhibits a continual succession of scenes of misery,
strife, and bloodshed, from which it is not possible
to infer that the human race will be any happier in
the future than it has been in the past. This poem
may be considered as the first of Thomson's in
which a wholly pessimistic view of human life was
taken by him ; and it has therefore an importance
which its merits otherwise would scarcely give it.

In 1863 the first of the poems which display the
great and peculiar genius of Thomson—namely, the
one entitled, "To our Ladies of Death "—appeared
in the *Reformer*. Perhaps I may be allowed to
mention here the fact that it was this poem which
first attracted my own attention to the writings of
" B. V.," and which convinced me that he was a
poet of no common order. I had about that time
become a subscriber to Mr. Bradlaugh's paper ;
and thenceforward I looked eagerly in its pages for
further contributions from the pen of the mysterious
" B. V.," who must be, I then thought, some well-
known poet of the time, veiling himself under those
initials.

It is unnecessary to mention here the various
writings of Thomson which made their first appearance in the *Reformer ;* but it may be stated
generally that much of his best work, both in prose
and verse, was first published in it. That his
writings in that paper, before the publication of
" The City of Dreadful Night," attracted no attention is not to be wondered at, for though the
Reformer was conducted with considerable ability,
and had many able contributors, it was not a
periodical in which one would have expected to
find such remarkable work as Thomson's. Its

readers were chiefly the more intelligent members
of the working classes, and these naturally were
more interested in the anti-theological and political
propaganda of the editor than in the more culti-
vated or scholarly articles of its (now) most distinguished writer. It was fortunate for Thomson
that the columns of his friend's paper were at all
times open to him : for in it he could publish without restraint his most heterodox essays, a privilege
which he could have enjoyed in no other journal of
that time. "Vane's Story" and "The City of
Dreadful Night" would have sought admission in
vain into the pages of any "respectable" contemporary periodical or magazine.

An event happened in 1862 which materially
altered Thomson's position and prospects. The
following passage from Mr. Salt's "Life of Thomson" gives a sufficient account of the circumstances :—

" In 1862, when his regiment was at Portsmouth, it
chanced that Thomson went on a visit to a fellow-
schoolmaster at Aldershot, and in the course of a stroll
in the neighbourhood of the camp one of the party, out
of bravado or for a wager, swam out to a boat which
was moored on a pond where boating was prohibited.
An officer demanded the names of those present, and
on this being refused further altercations followed, with
the result that a court-martial was held on the recal-
citrant schoolmasters. No real blame seems to have
attached to Thomson, but he paid the penalty of being
one of the incriminated party, and was discharged
from the service on October 30th, 1862."

Judging from this account the reader will probably
think that Thomson was very severely punished for a
small offence : but his great infirmity had, I believe,
already begun to show itself, and so it is probable
that the army authorities in discharging him were

not influenced solely by the ostensible cause. I
cannot but think that this was a most unfortunate
event for Thomson, for, irksome as his employment seemed to him, it was yet, like Lamb's clerk-
ship at the India House, a great steadying force,
and therefore a great blessing to him. All his
prospects were henceforth to be blighted by that
fatal disease which made the world for him an
Inferno, only less horrible than Dante's, because
the sufferings which he endured were not, as
he thought, inflicted upon him by an offended
deity, but by the blind action of unconscious forces.

On leaving the army Thomson applied to Mr,
Bradlaugh for assistance in his search for employment. It is due to the latter to say that he treated
his friend with much kindness and consideration.
He helped him to obtain various situations, and
moreover took him into his own household, where
for some years he remained as a member of the
family circle. In spite of his unfortunate failing
he was a great favourite with all the family, particularly with Mrs. Bradlaugh and her two daughters, one of whom has given an interesting account
of him as she knew him, and of the manner in
which he exerted himself to please and amuse her
and her sister.

From 1862 to 1869 Thomson endeavoured, with
almost uniform ill-success, to obtain admission for
some of his poems and prose writings to the pages
of the magazines of the time. Only in one important instance did he succeed. "Sunday up the
River" was published in *Fraser's Magazine*, Mr.
Froude, who was then the editor, having accepted
the poem after submitting it to Charles Kingsley,
who warmly recommended it. Froude, however,
declined afterwards to publish "Weddah and

Om-el-Bonain" in *Fraser*, and Thomson made no
further effort in that direction. He was, indeed,
quite destitute of that persistence and "push"
which enables some men of quite ordinary talents
to achieve a success which is often denied to those
of far greater powers.

In 1872 Thomson became the secretary of " The
Champion Gold and Silver Mines Company." In
this capacity he was sent out to America by the
directors to look after the company's interests.
How they came to select him for this duty it is
hard to conjecture, but doubtless they were un-
aware that he was a poet and a genius. However,
as the mine seems to have been one of the wild-cat
species, Thomson was probably as well-fitted to
look after it and to report upon its unproductive-
ness as a more practical expert would have been.
He remained in America about eight months, and
had a rather enjoyable time there, save that he was
laid up for some days by a rather sharp attack of
mountain fever. He returned to England in
January 1873, and the company being shortly
afterwards wound up, he was once more without
employment.

In July of this year he obtained (again through
Mr. Bradlaugh's recommendation) the post of
special correspondent of the *New York World* in
Spain, where a contest was then going on between
the Republican Government and the Carlists.
From an account of his experiences which Thomson afterwards gave in the *Secularist*, it appears
that the fighting was carried on in a very easy-
going way, neither party being too anxious to bring
the struggle to an end. They preferred, according
to the manner of the nation, not to fight to-day if
the contest could possibly be postponed to the

morrow. A Spaniard does not mind dying for his cause, but he will not abandon his leisurely habits for it. After Thomson had been in Spain about two months, during which time nothing that could furnish an excuse for a scare headline had occurred, his employers concluded that they were not getting value for their money, and so recalled their correspondent. Thomson was not an Archibald Forbes or an O'Donovan, but even they could not have made absorbingly interesting "copy" out of the events—or lack of events—of a struggle notable only for the unwillingness of the combatants to spoil sport by bringing it to a too-hasty conclusion.

With this experience what may be termed Thomson's active career terminated. Henceforth he became the literary man only, earning by his pen a scanty and precarious subsistence, and living a shadowed and dreamlike life, altogether alien to that of the great multitude around him.

It was in 1874 that the work which has proved to be his chief title to fame was first printed. On March 22, in that year, the first instalment of "The City of Dreadful Night" appeared in the *National Reformer*, and other portions appeared during April and May in the same paper. Not FitzGerald's "Omar Khayyam," which had been published about fifteen years before, and which was then just beginning to be talked about, stole into the world more noiselessly or seemed less likely to attract the world's attention and admiration than did Thomson's masterpiece. The fates of the two poems were indeed much alike. Both would have passed into complete oblivion but for the fact that they chanced to be seen by a few appreciative judges, who were able at last to persuade the reading public—or that small section of

it which cares for poetry—that though they had
been heralded by no flourish of trumpets, and
appealed to no popular sentiment, they must be
reckoned henceforth among the greatest poems of
the century.

Up to the appearance of "The City of Dreadful
Night" nothing that Thomson had published had
(save in one instance) attracted any kind of public
or even private notice. It would have been
strange, however, if so remarkable a work had
passed altogether unheeded. The *Academy* printed
an appreciative note — written by Miss Edith
Simcox—respecting it, quoting one of its sections
as an example of its remarkable qualities. This
reference induced a writer in the *Spectator* to
procure the poem, and to write an article upon it,
partly condemnatory it is true, but yet recognising
its great power. The author himself sent copies
of the poem to Carlyle, W. M. Rossetti, and
"George Eliot." From Carlyle he received no
response, but Mr. Rossetti, ever generous in his
appreciation of unknown or obscure merit, sent
him a letter of warm praise and encouragement.
From "George Eliot" he received a letter in which
she said that her mind responded with admiration
to the distinct vision and grand utterance in the
poem, but hoped that a mind informed with so
much passionate energy would soon produce works
with a wider embrace of human fellowship in them,
"such as will be to the labourers of the world what
the odes of Tyrtæus were to the Spartans, thrilling
them with the sublimity of the social order, and
the courage of resistance to all that would dissolve
it." Evidently the lady, while recognising the
power and sublimity of Thomson's chief work, was
a good deal disquieted by its intense pessimism.

He replied to her remarks in a letter which must be quoted, because in it he replies not only to her, but to a good many other critics who have since expressed similar opinions.

" DEAR MADAM,—Having been absent for several days, I am now only able to thank you for your very kind letter, for your generous expression of praise, and for your yet more generous expression of trust, though this, I fear, will prove to be misplaced.

"I have no Byronic quarrel with my fellows, whom I find all alike crushed under the iron yoke of Fate, and few of whom I can deem worse than myself, while so many are far better ; and I certainly have an affectionate and even joyful recognition of the willing labours of those who have striven to alleviate our lot, though I cannot see that all their efforts have availed much against the primal curse of our existence. Has the world been the better or the worse for the life of even such a man as Jesus ? I cannot judge ; but I fear on the whole considerably the worse. None the less I can love and revere his memory. A physician saves a life, and he does well ; yet perchance it were better for the patient and for others that he now died. But it is not for me to introduce such thoughts to you."

In a later note he gave a further explanation of his position :—

"In my note of Thursday I omitted to qualify, as I intended, the general statement by the distinct admission of what, however, is in all likelihood quite obvious —that the poem in question was the outcome of much sleepless hypochondria. I am aware that the truth of midnight does not exclude the truth of noonday, though one's nature may lead him to dwell in ¦the former rather than in the latter."

It was the appearance of "The City of Dreadful Night" in the *National Reformer* which led to my own acquaintance with the poet. I had been, as I have stated, a reader of the paper almost from its commencement, and I was always delighted whenever I found in it an article or a poem signed "B. V." When "The City" appeared, it was not published in successive numbers of the paper, the editor fearing perhaps that it might have too disturbing an effect upon the minds of his readers, unless care was taken to present it to them in not too frequent instalments. There was an interval of three weeks between the appearance of the first and the second portions of the poem. This led me to fear that it had been determined not to publish the remainder of it ; and I wrote to Mr. Bradlaugh to express my hope that no such decision had been come to. While doing so, I also took occasion to express my strong admiration of "B. V.'s" writings in general, and more particularly of his poetry. Mr. Bradlaugh handed my letter over to Thomson, who thereupon sent me the following letter :—

"DEAR SIR,—I have just received from Mr. Bradlaugh your note about myself, and hasten to thank you heartily for your very generous expression of approval of my writings. While I have neither tried nor cared to win any popular applause, the occasional approbation of an intelligent and sympathetic reader cheers me on a somewhat lonely path.

"You must not blame Mr. Bradlaugh for the delay in continuing my current contribution to his paper. He is my very dear friend, and always anxious to strain a point in my favour ; but as an editor he must try to suit his public, and the great majority of these care nothing for what I write. As for this 'City of Dreadful Night,' it is so alien from common thought and feeling, that I knew well (as stated in the Proem) that scarcely any readers would care for it, and Mr. Bradlaugh tells me that he has received three or four letters energetically protesting against its publication in the *N.R.*, yours, I think, being the only one praising it. Moreover, we must not forget that there is probably no other periodical in the kingdom which would accept such writings, even were their literary merits far greater than they are.

"I address from the office of the *N.R.* because I am just now rather unsettled, and not sure what will be my private address for some time to come. While preferring to remain anonymous for the public, I have no reason to hide my name from such correspondents as yourself.—I am, dear sir, yours truly,

"JAMES THOMSON (*B.V.*)."

In replying to this letter I expressed a wish to become personally acquainted with the writer. He was pleased to accede to my request, and thenceforth we remained on terms of friendship up to the time of his death. "Why don't you publish your poems in book form?" was naturally one of the first questions I put to him. In answer to this he explained that he thought it unlikely that any publisher could be found who would risk money in publishing them, and that he had no means of paying for their publication himself, as most modern poets have to do. This led me to make an offer of such assistance as might be within my power to give him. My first intention was to take the entire risk of the publication of a volume of his poems upon myself, but on going into the matter I found that the expense would be greater than I should be justified in incurring, considering my very limited means. This has ever since been a source of deep regret to me, and I have often reproached myself for not having had courage enough to run whatever risk there might then have been in publishing a volume of his poems. But I had been all my life up to that period extremely poor, and was then only just beginning to lift myself above the mere subsistence level. It is very hard, it has been said, to

eradicate the frost of poverty from the bones ; and
I believe few of those who have known the bitter-
ness of the struggle for a bare subsistence ever
succeed entirely in accomplishing it. Had I then
been able to publish "The City of Dreadful
Night," it might have saved him from five weary
years of poverty and obscurity, and might also have
had some influence in saving him from the consequences of his great infirmity. I say *might*, for
it is so impossible to say what might have occurred
if events had happened differently from what they
did, that it is conceivable that if Thomson's poems
had been issued then they might have attracted
little or no attention, and so their publication
would not have helped him. It requires, indeed, a
robust faith—a faith that will receive a good many
rude shocks—to believe, with Dr. Pangloss, that in
the life of man all things happen as they should
happen, at the right time and in the right way, and
neither too soon nor too late ; yet, looking at the
course my own life has taken, I have sometimes
been tempted to think that such a belief is not
without warrant. But one person's experience—
though no doubt mine has not been altogether un-
paralleled—cannot avail against the weight of
evidence which seems to tell in favour of the
contrary belief. To discuss such a question here,
however, would be going too far afield : the bio-
grapher's concern is with what did happen, and not
with what might have happened.

In justice to myself I must say that I made
several efforts on Thomson's behalf to procure the
publication of his poems, before I did at last
succeed in my efforts. On one occasion I brought
about an interview between him and a well-known
poet, who afterwards succeeded to a title, and who

had expressed an interest in Thomson and a desire
to help him—a desire, however, which did not
eventually express itself in anything beyond words.
He was a most amiable and well-meaning man,
but, like most poets, was vastly more interested in
his own verses than in those of any other author.
I do not know of any poets of the last century who
were willing to sacrifice time or money in favour of
a less fortunate singer than themselves, save
Shelley, Sydney Dobell, and Lord Houghton. I
am afraid that most poets are very pronounced
egoists, and find much difficulty in believing that
any contemporary of theirs can have any claim to
attention which can compare in any degree with
their own.

Early in 1875 some disagreements occurred
between the editor of the *National Reformer* and
his most brilliant contributor. This led to Thomson's secession from the paper, and to a state of
permanent antagonism between the former friends.
Into the reasons which led to this antagonism I
will not enquire too curiously, but I fear that
Thomson's unfortunate failing was at least partly
responsible for it. Bradlaugh, to do him justice,
had up to this time exhibited a great deal of
patience and forbearance in his dealings with his
gifted friend. Like most men, Bradlaugh had his
faults, but he was a good and generous friend ; and
he would not, I think, have broken with Thomson
had he not had sufficient reasons for so doing.
Thomson, however, considered himself to have
been badly treated, and thereafter, whenever he
referred to his former friend, expressed himself in a
tone of much asperity. He always attributed the
breach between them to the influence which a well-
known lady, who was then associated with Brad-

laugh in his political and anti-theological work, had gained over the great agitator.

Being no longer employed upon the *Reformer*, it was now necessary for Thomson to seek for other means of existence; and it was fortunate for him that through the introduction of his friend, William Maccall, he was able to obtain another engagement which was, during the few years he was yet to live, to prove his main support. Messrs. Cope, the well-known tobacco merchants of Liverpool, published at this time a monthly periodical called *Cope's Tobacco Plant*. This was, no doubt, intended chiefly as an advertising medium for their business: but it was nevertheless a well-written and entertaining miscellany. Many well-known writers contributed to its pages, and there is much matter in it which might very well be collected and published in book-form. Its editor was the late Mr. John Fraser, one of the best of Scotsmen, and the most kind and generous of men. The contributors were paid on a very liberal scale, and Thomson, I believe, gained more from his connexion with it than from any other of his literary engagements. To its pages he contributed articles on Ben Jonson, Rabelais, John Wilson, James Hogg, and Walt Whitman: also reviews of books, a series of papers on tobacco legislation, etc. He was one of its most constant contributors from 1875 until 1881, when, unfortunately for him, it was discontinued.

In January, 1876, a new Freethought paper was started under the joint editorship of Messrs. G. W. Foote and G. J. Holyoake. With the former he had for some two or three years previously been on somewhat intimate terms, Mr. Foote having a great admiration for his writings. Thomson was glad therefore to become a contributor to the new paper; and during its continuance he wrote for it more industriously and on more various subjects than for any other periodical. Anyone who now looks through a file of the paper can hardly fail to be impressed with a sense of the versatility of his powers. There is a disposition on the part of some of his critics to assert that his talents were confined within a very limited range, and more than one of them has expressed the opinion that "The City of Dreadful Night" is the only one of his works which posterity will care for. No one who reads through his writings in the *Secularist* can entertain that idea. One of his most important contributions to it was a series of articles on Heinrich Heine, who (after Shelley) was the author with whom Thomson was most in sympathy, and whom he had most thoroughly studied. It is generally acknowledged that the spirit and music of the lyrics of the German poet have been more adequately rendered into English by Thomson than by any other translator. One of the projects which were cut short by his untimely death was a book on Heine which he had undertaken to write.

From 1874 to the time of his death a good deal of correspondence passed between the poet and myself. I will now quote a few passages, such as have a general or personal interest, from his letters.

On June 24, 1874, after referring to the notice in the *Academy* of "The City of Dreadful Night," he adds:— *223975*

"I have just written to the editor, thanking him and his critic, and saying that it seems to me a very brave act on the part of a respectable English periodical to spontaneously call attention to an atheistical writing (less remote than, say, Lucretius), treating it simply or solely on its literary merits without obloquy or protesting cant."

The following passage from a letter dated January 9, 1876, should, I think, be carefully noted, since it gives Thomson's answer not only to Mr. Bullen's censures on his use of various uncommon words or phrases in his verse, but also to similar expressions of opinion from various other critics :—

"With regard to Mr. A. H. Bullen's criticisms on 'Our Ladies of Death'—criticisms which really flatter me, as any man's work is really praised by such examination—I must hold myself right. The only English dictionary I have by me is a school one, but as such little likely to venture on neologisms ; moreover, it is very good of its kind, being Reid's of Edinburgh. This gives Sombre : sombrous, dark, gloomy ; Tenebrous — Tenebrious : dark, gloomy, obscure (and of course Tenebrious implies Tenebriously) ; Ruth : pity, sorrow ; Ruthful : merciful, sorrowful ; Ruthfully : sadly, sorrowfully. The huge Worcester Webster, into which I looked a day or two after your letter came, agrees as to Tenebrious and Ruth ; I forgot to look in it for Sombrous. But as to Ruth, I used it in the common sense of pity, not that of sadness and sorrow. When I wrote—

> ' My life but bold
> In jest and laugh to parry hateful ruth,'

I meant, to parry the pity of others, not to parry my own sadness, which indeed jest and laugh must intensify instead of 'parrying.' My thought was much like that of Beatrice, *The Cenci*, Act v., Sc. 3 :—

> ' Shall the light multitude
> Fling at their choice curses or *faded pity*,
> Sad funeral flowers to deck a living corpse
> Upon us as we pass, to pass away ?'

And from the light indifferent multitude, as you must

know, curses are even less unwelcome than pity when we are profoundly suffering. I looked into the dictionaries not knowing whether their authority would sustain or condemn me, as I am used to trust in careful writing to my own sense of what is right ; this, naturally, having been modified and formed by reading of good authors. Even had the dictionaries condemned me, I should in these cases have been apt to assert my own correctness ; in many others I should be ready to yield without contest. In 'The City of Dreadful Night,' I used tenebrous instead of tenebrious ; just as good writers use, as it happens to suit them, either funeral or funereal, sulphurous or sulphureous (Shelley often in *Hellas*), &c. You will think I have troubled you with many words on a very little matter. . . . . As it is now just eleven p.m., and I have much to do to-morrow, I will conclude in pity for myself if not in ruth for you."

The following passage is extracted from a letter dated March 7, 1877 :—

" That notice about publication of my poems in the *Academy* was rather premature, nor was I aware that it was going to be inserted. After keeping me waiting for months, and saying there was no objection to the publication, King's* have asked me to release them from promise to publish. Real reason, we may presume, they funked — being, perhaps, especially timorous just now with the *Nineteenth Century* and *Contemporary* row on. I let Paul † understand that I considered myself treated badly."

Under date February 12, 1878, he writes :—

" I have called at Trübner's about poems. Trübner himself on the Continent, but I saw his partner, Edwardes. He, like Chatto and Windus, told me that trade was so depressed that they are withholding several works ready for publication. If the damned

---

* Messrs. Henry S. King & Co.
† The late Mr. Kegan Paul.

Dizzy suspense be over, and trade improved, will be happy to see me on the subject in June, when they make their arrangements for works to be brought out in the following season, which, as you doubtless know, begins with November. There would be no fair chance for a volume now. So I must wait once more."

The following passage is from a letter dated November 1, 1878 :—

"I am very sorry, but scarcely surprised, that things are not very flourishing with you just now. You are correct in supposing that it is ditto with me. With the natural depression of trade infinitely aggravated during the past two years by the infernal impolicy of our Jewish-Jingo misgovernment, it cannot be well with anybody but arms-manufacturers, exchange-speculators, and Hebrew adventurers, and things seem likely to get much worse before they get better. From your address I fear that you have been obliged to give up your Edgware-road business. As for me, I am still depending solely on Fraser. Many thanks for the 'Whiffs of Smoke' concerning which I write to that good gentleman. The 'Improvisations'* I shall be delighted to see. It is at

---

* This refers to a volume of poems by Dr. Garth Wilkinson, entitled, "Improvisations from the Spirit," which the author claims to have written without premeditation or conscious effort on his part, he being merely the medium of communication in the matter. On this all that need be said is that the poems do not exhibit any peculiarities which cannot be imagined to have had their origin in Dr. Wilkinson's own mind, quite unaided by any extraneous power. The book is interesting from the fact that it is the only one of its kind in the English language, though improvised poems and dramas are (or were) common enough in Italy. But if the English language were as flexible, and as prolific in rhymes, as the Italian, improvisation, I suppose, would be as common with us as with them. What is done with facility, however, is seldom done well, and so it is not to be regretted that improvisation in English verse is almost unknown. I do not

any rate so scarce that I have never yet been able to come across it, and have never seen any mention of it save that by D. G. Rossetti in his supplementary chapter (a very fine one) to the 'Life of Blake.' It is not even in the British Museum, having been printed for private circulation only, if I remember aright. I should think it would be a real treasure to any of Wilkinson's few admirers ; for, as you know, the fewer the devotees of any man, or thing, the more enthusiastic."

The following extract is from a letter dated December 23, 1878 :—

" Many thanks for the 'Improvisations,' which, however, I can only accept if the volume, being less rare than I had supposed, does not command a high price. . . . . A brief glance at it, and perusal of the remarkable note at the end, make me anticipate its study with unusual interest.

" Just lately, and in these days, I am pretty busy for Fraser, and well for me that it is so, for I have not earned a penny save from him the whole year. There is more work to do on the Tobacco Duties ; and also verse and prose for the Xmas Card, but not so much as last year, nor offering such genial opportunities and associations as Chaucer's Canterbury Pilgrims.* The subject this time is the Pursuit of Diva Nicotina, in imitation of Sir Noel Paton's Pursuit of Pleasure. Paton is a good poet and painter too, but of the ascetic-pietistic school, or with strong leanings to it.

" Like yourself, I am anything but sanguine of the

---

think that, even in Italian, any work of real merit has been produced in that way. Easily-written verse, it has been said, makes "damned hard reading," but this perhaps is more epigrammatic than true. It may in some cases be as easily read as written ; but then it is also just as easily forgotten.

* This refers to two large coloured plates which were issued with the *Tobacco Plant*, and for which Thomson wrote explanatory and descriptive matter in verse and prose.

success of *The Liberal*,* and have always discouraged
Foote from it.   I would really prefer having nothing
to do with it, though it will bring me a little money
while it lasts; but I could not well refuse contributions
when pressed."

From a later dated October 19, 1879, the following passages are taken :—

" Like yourself, I can still but barely manage to
keep head above water—sometimes sinking under for
a bit.   You see what I do for Cope.   I have not
succeeded in getting any other work except on *The
Liberal*, and this is of small value. . . . . I thank you
for keeping the Whitman† for me.   I sold it with other
books when hard up.   In the meantime I have the
latest 2 vol. edition in hand from Fraser, who has
requested some articles on him when Tobacco Legislation, etc., will allow.   I mean to begin him now in
the evenings at home, as the Legislation can be done
only in the Museum.   He may occupy such intervals
in the paper as did the Wilson and Hogg, both done
by request : the 'Richard Feverel' was on my own
suggestion.   George Meredith, to whom I sent a copy,
wrote me a very flattering, because very high-minded,
letter.   He has seen the 'City,' and though by no
means sanguine with such a public as ours, he thinks it
should float a volume.   The admiration of so many
good literary judges really surprises me."

During the seven years following the composition
of "The City of Dreadful Night," Thomson had

---

* This was a monthly magaziné which was then about to
be published.   It was ably edited by Mr. Foote, and had
many talented contributors, but met with the usual fate of
such ventures, running to twelve numbers only.   Thomson
contributed to it a good many articles, the most notable of
which was one upon the already-mentioned "Improvisations" by Dr. Wilkinson.

† Whitman's "Leaves of Grass."

ceased almost entirely to write verse. This was no
doubt partly owing to his absorption in journalistic
work, but much more to the want of encouragement and appreciation which he had met with.
There was only one noteworthy exception to his
silence as a poet during these "seven songless
years," as he himself called them. During the
evenings of September 16, 17, and 18, 1878, he
was engaged in the composition of a poem which
is still in manuscript, because it was one of the
author's last desires that it should not be published.
I regret this very much because, in view of its
autobiographical interest and importance, its sup-
pression is certainly a thing to be regretted. The
author, however, only objected to its publication
because he thought it defective in literary form,
and not because of its subject. His own words
with respect to it are that he considered it "too
hard and harsh in both conception and execution
for attempt at polishing—far more truth than poetry
in it." I think then that though I cannot publish
the poem in its complete form—as I should like to
do—there can be no harm in giving a summary of
its contents, together with a few quotations from it.
What follows, then, is a brief account of the poem
in which, more plainly than in any other, Thomson
expressed his inmost thoughts and feelings.
Whether he did in this poem really succeed in
expressing the "true truth" about himself may
possibly be questioned, since all men are liable to
self-deception; but it is certain at least that the
poet's analysis of his own mind and heart may be
accepted as a wholly sincere representation of what
he himself believed to be the truth; whether it
represents the whole truth I will not now stop to
enquire.

> " I had a Love : it was so long ago,
>   So many long sad years :
> She died—and then a waste of arid woe,
>   Never refreshed by tears :
> She died so young, so tender, pure and fair :
> I wandered in the Desert of Despair."

What then kept him from following his dead love,
and led him still to tread the barren ways of life?
What drugged his keen intent to sink or soar in the
dark abyss of death?   How has he existed so long
with no well-spring of comfort for his soul, no
aliment for his forlorn heart, and without the
support of Faith, Hope, and Love?   His heart, he
answers, has fed upon itself, "the bitter, poisoned
meat," his soul has drunk its own scant fountains
dry, and his feet have year by year circled in their
old footsteps in the drear desert of life.   He plods
for ever upon burning sands and bruising stones,
and all he sees are the dry bleached bones of men
and camels, and vultures watching for their prey.
He himself would fain lie down and become a part
of the carrion banquet, but some unblessed goad
debars him from such long-wished-for rest.

> " Songs in the desert ! Songs of husky breath !
>   And undivine despair ;
> Songs that are Dirges, but for Life not Death ;
>   Songs that infect the air
> Have sweetened bitterly my food and wine,
> The heart corroded and the Dead Sea brine."

Yet, so potent with us is the Word; and Art, which
urges us to perpetual strife with Death, is so
tenacious that their magic can keep us living in
our own despite.   How strange that we can con-
front the direst woes if only we may have the poor
relief of uttering our sorrow in the form of music,
painting, sculpture, verse or prose !   The splen-
dours of creative art cleave the sepulchral glooms

of death, and revive the ancient dead : lowly tombs
become by its aid grand palaces :—

> " Funereal black to royal purple glows,
> And corpses stand up kings from long repose."

And yet not a night has passed since she was
lost to him that he would not have welcomed
with serene delight the command, " Go sleep, go
sleep, thy long day's travail done ! " How fer-
vently, while yet he half-believed that she was a
radiant spirit by the Heavenly Throne, did his
weak and selfish heart pray that she might return
to him and change his weary moans to hymns' of
triumph and enraptured love ! But now, when he
sees that Immortality is but a vain dream, and that
she, his dead love, is indeed lost to him for ever,
since at death all mankind are resolved into the
Universe from which they are so mysteriously
evolved—now when it is apparent to him that all
the races of man are but as mites in infinities of
Time and Space, and that our earth is but as a

> " Many-insect-peopled drop of dew
> Exhaling in a moment from the view "—

now that by grievous thought he has learned something of the truth about Life and Death and about
himself – if now he found that there is indeed a
living God, and he were to hear His voice proclaim
that his dead love should be restored, and that she
should return to him as young and fair as when she
died, and that he also should be restored to youth
and vigour, and that then they should lead a long
and happy life together in a home brightened with
the faces of joyous children—even then he would
reply, " Lord of the Universe, pity and pardon me,
I shudder from this blessing as a curse, and sup-
plicate Thee not to alter our fate. For she now

enjoys eternal rest, and I too am near the shore of that eternity wherein all woes are ended."

> " I would not tear her from her resting-place
>   For any human bliss ;
> I would not one of my past years retrace
>   Who seek the black abyss ;
> I would not have the burden on my soul
> Of bringing babes into this world of dole."

It gives him solace now instead of grief to brood over her fate and murmur :—

> " She died so young, so tender, pure, and fair."

And now, too, his own good time cannot be long delayed. How piteous is life, and how sublime is death ! For what purpose was the human race created ?

> " What profit from all life that lives on earth,
>   What good, what use, what aim ?
> What compensation for the throes of birth
>   And death in all its frame ?
> What conscious life hath ever paid its cost ?
> From Nothingness to Nothingness—all lost ! "

So ends this remarkable poem, than which, though it lacks the poet's last touches, and is therefore not so perfect in form as the author could easily have made it, no more pathetic and heart-moving expression of desolation of spirit and hopeless despair has ever yet been uttered by poet or musician.

There is a strange supplement or postscript to the poem, which is too characteristic not to be quoted here. It is as follows :—

"Writing the foregoing lines, I have felt like a man making his will at the gates of Death, summing up Life's scores and settling accounts when about to leave its inn. Yet I do not truly feel very near to Death, for with a seeming partial revival of the

creative energies in thought and imagination, it is
impossible to realise death, even when absorbed by its
sombre fascination.   It may be merely the throes of
some new birth that give the lethal illusion ; for birth
is so like death.

> ' I do not hate a single man alive,
>   Some few I must disdain ;
> I have loved heartily some four or five,
>   And of these there remain
> Just two, I think, for whom I would outface
> Death gladly ; for the one death and disgrace.' "

Among the four or five friends whom he had loved
heartily, we may be sure that Mr. and Mrs. Barnes
were included ; but they were, I believe, both dead
at the time the verses were written.   As to the
persons to whom he alludes in the final couplet,
though a guess at their identity might be hazarded,
it could be no more than a guess.

From the mood of utter hopelessness into which
the poet had fallen, he was now to be for a
brief period uplifted.   Early in 1880, a fortunate
inspiration led me to make an application on
Thomson's behalf to Messrs. Reeves & Turner,
the well-known booksellers and publishers, who
then had an establishment in the Strand, next door
to the office of *The Illustrated London News.*   Here
I must pay ·a passing tribute of respect and gratitude to the memory of the leading partner of the
firm, Mr. William Reeves, one of the kindest, most
honourable, and most loveable of men, of whom it
might truly be said that no one could know him
without having a warm feeling of affection for him.
It was to him that I made my application, and on
the faith of his confidence in my judgment, he at
once agreed to bring out, at our joint risk, a volume
of Thomson's poems.   I explained to him that the
heterodox   character   of   Thomson's   verse   had

hitherto proved the chief obstacle in the way of
its publication ; but he was not disposed to allow
such a consideration to influence him. The work
therefore was at once put in hand, and in June,
1880, "The City of Dreadful Night, and other
Poems" was published. Its reception was, upon
the whole, as good as could have been expected.
A poem which ran so counter to the general current
of opinion of its time—for the new theologians had
not then discovered how to remain Christians while
discarding almost every distinctive doctrine of the
Christian faith—could not hope for a warm
welcome from the orthodox organs of opinion, but
the more purely literary papers received it with
a good deal of respect, though with no great en-
thusiasm.* The most generous and unstinted
recognition of the interest and importance of the
book was made in an article headed "A New
Poet," which appeared in the *Fortnightly Review*,
then under the editorship of John Morley.† This
was written by Mr. G. A. Simcox, a discerning
critic, and something of a poet himself. If he did
not commit himself to any very warm eulogium of
Thomson's work, he showed by his careful analysis
of its qualities and characteristics, that he regarded
the new poet as one who was to be counted among

---

* It must be admitted, however, that it was much more
favourably received than was Fitzgerald's "Omar Khayyam"
on its first appearance in print. Whether that poem received
any notice at all from the Press I do not know ; but it is
certain that it did not receive any such notice as could have
induced more than a few—a very few—readers to purchase it.

† It is worth noting that George Meredith asked Mr. Morley
to allow him to review the book in the *Fortnightly ;* but the
latter could not accept the offer because he had already
engaged Mr. Simcox to do it.

the master-singers of the time, whatever shortcomings in him might be detected by a critical
scrutiny of his writings. As the critic gave many
illustrative extracts from the poems, his article was
well calculated to excite the reader's interest in the
poet, and to convince him that James Thomson
was not merely one of the "new poets" who were
just then rather plentiful, but one who was
destined, unlike the others, to achieve a lasting
reputation.* Other critics were not so discerning as Mr. Simcox, though in only one or
two cases, I believe, did they fail altogether
to recognise the power and significance of
Thomson's work. Naturally enough, the intense
gloom and hopelessness of the leading poem
proved so distasteful to some of the reviewers
that they were unable or unwilling to do justice to
its great qualities. One acute critic, whose pene-
tration is not usually so much at fault, gave it as
his opinion that the gloom and hopelessness of the
poem did not represent the author's real feelings,
but were merely assumed in accordance with the
then prevailing poetical fashion. So inept a criticism must have been received by Thomson with
a scornful smile, for if ever there was a work which
expressed with entire sincerity its Author's mind
and feelings, that work was "The City of Dreadful
Night." We may indeed dissent from its conclusions, and say that it gives a morbid and untrue
picture of human life, because it leaves out of

---

* Perhaps it may be worth while to remark that though
Thomson was to the critics and the public of the time a
"new" poet, he was not so in fact, being in reality a
contemporary of Swinburne, Rossetti, Morris, and Arnold ;
though all these had won fame and recognition a good many
years before Thomson got his chance.

account the compensating elements which do at
least make it endurable to the great majority of
mankind : but that to Thomson, as to Leopardi
and Schopenhauer, it did really appear to be the
evil and accursed thing which he has represented
it to be, can never again be doubted.   Let it be
granted that the intense hopelessness of the poem
was the expression of a mind naturally prone to
gloom and melancholy, and that it might therefore
be answered by producing evidence that some few
mortals at least have been happy in their lives, and
have found the world to be no ill abiding place,
it yet remains to be decided whether there is not,
upon the whole, a great preponderance of evil over
good in the life of man, and whether the optimist,
who sees only the bright side of things, is not even
more seriously at fault than the pessimist, who can
see no good whatever in it.   If I were asked for
my own opinion upon the matter, I think I should
reply that the whole truth is neither with the
optimist nor the pessimist ; but that though it is
impossible to deny that there are many evils which
are inseparable from human life, there are, nevertheless, sufficient compensations for those evils to
make life at least supportable for the major part of
mankind, though not for those afflicted with too
quick sensibilities, or who are too acutely alive to
the injustice, the brutality, and the suffering which
they see around them.   Happily for most people,
their sensibilities are infinitely less acute than those
of a Pascal, a Leopardi, or a Thomson.   Life, it
would seem, can only be enjoyed on condition that
we refrain from thinking about it, even as the
lower animals do.   " Nothing is good or bad but
thinking makes it so ; " and the writer who has
recently urged that man's unhappiness really

springs from the fact that nature accidentally bestowed upon him a brain larger than he required to fit him for the place for which he was designed, is not, I think, without good warrant for his opinion. Every animal but man is fitted exactly for its place, and has a brain and organisation such as enables it perfectly to fulfil its allotted part in the scheme of nature. Man alone is dissatisfied with his lot because he alone realises that life has no prizes with which to reward him for his ceaseless toils and his continual sufferings.

With the man of genius—or at least with most men of genius—"every experience is so keen that mind and body are alike exhausted, and the will succumbs before the mere process of living." Yet it is just this excessive sensibility which is the necessary condition of their art. Their physical and mental powers are often too feeble to withstand the strain of the creative effort. Hence the frequent attacks of depression and melancholia from which they suffer ; and sometimes their pessimism. It is impossible, however, to treat pessimism as a mere outcome of a diseased or defective physical organisation. There are times when all men are pessimists, since all men suffer at some time from grief, anxiety, or physical or mental suffering. It cannot be denied, I think, that the pessimist at least makes out a strong case for his conclusions ; and the only way of answering him, so far as I can see, is to urge that though there may be some truth in his contentions, it is yet not the whole truth. Were life wholly evil it must soon cease to exist, for it would necessarily destroy itself. So far, then, as art is concerned, the conclusion surely is that the poet must be left to express himself according to his own temperament, no matter whether that temperament inclines him to an optimistic or pessimistic view of life or nature. It has been said that there can be no justification for the writing of such a poem as the " City of Dreadful Night," because the poet's object should be to increase the sum of human happiness, and not to render man's existence yet more insupportable. But a view of the poet's office which reduces him to a mere purveyor of mental syrup for the benefit of the soft-headed and soft-hearted will hardly commend itself to a robust intelligence. If Shakespeare was justified in writing " King Lear " or " Hamlet," then Thomson was no less justified in writing " The City of Dreadful Night." If ever any man was born to accomplish a particular task, Thomson was born for the purpose of writing his great masterpiece, and he would have lived in vain had he failed to write it. It is the one great and final poetic expression of pessimistic thought, and as such it must ever remain an unique and unsurpassable achievement.

What perhaps gave Thomson the keenest pleasure in connexion with the publication of his first volume, was the reception of a letter from George Meredith, in acknowledgment of a copy of the book which the author had sent him. Thomson had, some few months earlier, had some correspondence with Meredith, for whose writings he had the deepest admiration—an admiration which he had taken more than one opportunity of expressing. In July, 1879, Meredith wrote thus to Thomson :—

" I am glad to be in personal communication with you. The pleasant things you have written of me could not be other than agreeable to a writer. I saw

that you had the rare deep love of literature : rare at
all times, and in our present congestion of matter,
almost extinguished ; which led you to recognise any
effort to produce the worthiest. But when a friend
unmasked your initials, I was flattered. For I had
read 'The City of Dreadful Night,' and to be
praised by the author of that poem would strike all
men able to form a judgment upon eminent work, as
a distinction."

Here is the letter which Meredith wrote to
Thomson on April 27, 1880, after reading the
latter's first volume :—

"I will not delay any longer to write to you on the
subject of your book, though I am not yet in a
condition to do justice either to the critic or the poet,
for, owing to the attack I suffered under last year, I
have been pensioned off all work of any worth of late ;
and in writing to you about this admirable and price-
less book of verse, I have wished to be competent to
express my feeling for your merit, and as much as
possible the praise of such rarely-equalled good work.
My friends could tell you that I am a critic hard
to please. They say that irony lurks in my eulogy.
I am not, in truth, frequently satisfied by verse. Well,
I have gone through your volume—and partly a second
time—and I have not found the line I would propose
to recast. I have found many pages that no other
English poet could have written. Nowhere is the
verse feeble, nowhere is the expression insufficient ;
the majesty of the line has always its full colouring,
and marches under a banner. And you accomplish
this effect with the utmost sobriety, with absolute self-
mastery. I have not time at present to speak of the
City of Melencolia. There is a massive impressive-
ness in it that goes beyond Dürer, and takes it into
upper regions where poetry is the sublimation of the
mind of man, the voice of our highest. What might
have been said contra poet, I am glad that you should
have forestalled and answered in 'Philosophy'—very
wise writing. I am in love with the dear London lass

who helped you to the 'Idyll of Cockaigne.' You give a zest and new attraction to Hampstead Heath."

A nobler or more generous tribute from poet to poet was surely never given than this. It is the more noteworthy, because other contemporary poets, some of whom, at least, recognised the greatness of Thomson's work, were very chary of giving expression to their admiration of it. One of the most distinguished of them, after bestowing the most enthusiastic praise upon "Weddah and Om-el-Bonain," thought proper afterwards to withdraw it on the plea that Thomson, in some of his other writings, had gone somewhat too far in his attacks upon the popular faith—a sufficiently surprising pronouncement from such a quarter! But Meredith, besides being the sanest and manliest of writers, was also the manliest of men, and did not fear to express his admiration of a man or a poet because he was not counted among the ranks of the respectable or the well-connected.

With the publication of his first volume, Thomson had arrived at the culminating point of his career. His constitution, originally robust and better fitted than most men's to endure the wear and tear of life, but now undermined by the pressure of grief and hopelessness, and by his indulgence in the stimulants in which he found a temporary but costly relief, began now to break down so rapidly as to render illusory the brighter prospect which the success of his first volume of poems seemed to have opened before him. He was, indeed, yet to enjoy some brief periods of comparative happiness; and, what was even more surprising, his poetical genius was again to shine forth in its full lustre; but his good fortune came much too late—if, indeed, it could ever have come early enough—to save him from the consequences of the evil fate which had doomed him from his birth to wither under the conviction that life held nothing good for him, and that he was predestined to defeat in all his undertakings.   The fable of the prince on whom, at his birth, the good fairies lavished their choicest gifts, which were all to be rendered unavailing by the one evil gift of the malicious fairy, received, in his case, one more illustration to be added to the innumerable instances of which all history and biography are full.

The success of " The City of Dreadful Night " led to the issue, in the following October, of " Vane's Story, Om-el-Bonain, and other Poems " ; and this was followed in 1881 by the publication of a volume of his prose writings under the title of " Essays and Phantasies." These two books, which, with his first volume, were the only ones published during the author's lifetime, met with a very moderate measure of success. " Vane's Story," it is true, was, on the whole, favourably reviewed, though some critics, strangely enough, found even more fault with it on account of its anti-theological bias than they had done with the terrible " City." What was surprising, however, was the fact that " Essays and Phantasies," that splendid volume of prose, packed full of keen thought, fine criticism, and admirable writing, received scarcely any notice from the leading organs of critical opinion, and was almost a failure as a publishing venture. Not much more than three hundred copies of the book had been disposed of when, in 1890 (nine years after its first issue), the remaining copies, together with the stock of Thomson's other books, were destroyed by fire.* Thomson the poet has, up to the present, overshadowed Thomson the prose writer; but I cannot doubt that justice will ultimately be done to him in both capacities.

Towards the end of June, 1880, George Meredith invited Thomson to spend a day with him at his residence at Boxhill. " Last Tuesday," he wrote to me, " I spent with Meredith ; a real red-letter day in all respects. He is one of those personalities who need fear no comparison with their best writings."

In a letter to me, dated January 5, 1881, he writes :—

" With Mr. Wright and Percy [Holyoake] I went to George Eliot's funeral. It was wretched tramping through the slush, and then standing in the rain for about three-quarters of an hour, with nothing to see but dripping umbrellas. I was disappointed at there being any chapel service at all. At the grave, old Dr. Sadler mumbled something, of which only two or three words could be distinguished by us, only a couple of yards behind him."

Early in 1881, Thomson, who had already visited Leicester, and made there a number of good and generous friends, was invited to write an " Address " in verse to be recited at the opening of the New Hall of the Leicester Secular Society, and also to be present on the occasion of its delivery. These requests he willingly acceded to ; and on March 5 he travelled, in company with

---

* It is surely something of a reflection upon the public taste, that the publishers of Thomson's works have not, up to the present time, received sufficient encouragement to issue a second edition of the book. It is hoped, however, that a re-issue of it, forming part of a complete edition of Thomson's works, may shortly be undertaken.

Mr. and Mrs. Wright, to Leicester, where he stayed, enjoying the hospitality of several friends, for the next four days. On this occasion he first made the acquaintance of Mr. John W. Barrs, who was henceforth to prove one of his most devoted admirers and most generous friends. On June 4 in the same year, Thomson again went to Leicester, having been invited thither by a number of the friends whose hospitality he had enjoyed on his previous visit. The following extract from his diary sums up the story of his stay there on this occasion :—

"To Leicester on June 4th with the Wrights and Adeline [Holyoake]. Myself kept out of town seven weeks—one week at Quorndon with Phil Wright and brothers ; three days in Leicester with Mr. Michael Wright ; one day with Mr. Gimson ; all the other five-and-a-half weeks with the Barrs at Forest Edge, Kirby Muxloe, four miles out of Leicester. Unbounded hospitality : splendid holiday."

The seven weeks of this sojourn with his Leicester friends was, I believe, the pleasantest and happiest period of the poet's later life. Though it may seem apparently to contradict the whole tenor of the present narrative, it is nevertheless the fact that few men have ever had a greater capacity for enjoyment than he had, or could contribute more largely to the enjoyment of others when circumstances were favourable. Let me quote on this point the words of his friend, Mr. J. W. Barrs :—

"Whatever has been said or written of his charm of manner and conversation, has not and cannot give a just representation of them. Few men have known so delightful a friend, and his hilarity could equal his sombreness when in congenial company. One could hardly say more to anyone who knows 'The City of Dreadful Night.' The poem, 'At Belvoir,' recalls three days of incessant mirth and midsummer pleasure, Thomson being chief jester."

From the poem, " At Belvoir," which was written in January, 1882, but which refers to the occurrences of Sunday, July 11, 1881, and which hints at a last romance of love in the poet's life— a romance that possibly might have had a happy termination, if he could even then have regained his power of self-control—I must quote four or five significant stanzas :—

> " My thoughts go back to last July,
>   Sweet happy thoughts and tender ;—
> ' The bridal of the earth and sky,'
>   A day of noble splendour ;
> A day to make the saddest heart
>   In joy a true believer ;
> When two good friends we roamed apart
>   The shady walks of Belvoir.
>
> A maiden like a blushing rose,
>   Unconscious of the golden
> And fragrant bliss of love that glows
>   Deep in her heart infolden ;
> A Poet old in years and thought,
>   Yet not too old for pleasance,
> Made young again and fancy-fraught
>   By such a sweet friend's presence.
>
> *   *   *   *   *
>
> We roamed with many a merry jest,
>   And many a ringing laughter ;
> The slow calm hours too rich in zest
>   To heed before and after :
> Yet lingering down the lovely walks
>   Soft strains anon came stealing,
> A finer music in our talks
>   Of sweeter deeper feeling.
>
> *   *   *   *   *

My thoughts go on to next July,
  More happy thoughts, more tender ;
' The bridal of the earth and sky,'
  A day of perfect splendour ;
A day to make the saddest heart
  In bliss a firm believer ;
When two True Loves may roam apart
  The shadiest walks of Belvoir.

There may be less of merry jest,
  And less of ringing laughter,
Yet life be much more rich in zest,
  And richer still thereafter ;
The love-scenes of that region fair
  Have very real rehearsing,
And tremulous kisses thrill the air
  Far sweetlier than sweet versing."

Alas ! the poet in this case was but a false
prophet, and before the coming of that July here
so joyously anticipated, he was to find—where only
it was possible for him to find it—peace and rest
in the arms of "dateless oblivion and divine
repose." Before relating the infinitely sad and
terrible end of the poet's career, let me give, from
one of his letters to me, a last glimpse of the
gleam of happiness which he enjoyed with his
Leicester friends :—

" We are here four miles from Leicester, with rail-
way station a few minutes off, in a pleasant villa,
surrounded by shrubbery, lawn, meadow, and kitchen
garden. Host and hostess (sister) are kindness itself,
as are all other Leicester friends. We live the most
healthy of lives, save for strong temptations to over-
feeding on excellent fare, and host's evil and power-
fully contagious habit of sitting up till about 2 a.m.,
smoking, or reading and chatting. I now leave him
to his own wicked devices at midnight, or as soon
after as possible. Despite the showery weather, we
have had good drives and walks (country all green
and well-wooded), jolly little picnics, and lawn-tennis

ad infinitum. (N.B.—Lawn-tennis, even more than lady's fine pen, responsible for the uncouthness of this scrawl.) In brief, we have been so busy with enjoyment that this is the first note I have accomplished (or begun) in the seventeen days. I say *we*, because Adeline [Holyoake] is still here. She leaves about end of week, and I shall then spend a week at Quorndon, where three of Mr. Wright's sons live, managing the factories there. Thence I return here for two or three days, and perhaps shall spend two or three with old Mr. Wright before homing. You see I mean to have a good holiday before setting to work again."

It is with no common degree of pain that I now turn my thoughts towards the last portion of my task. In the annals of literature, wherein so many tragedies are recorded, there is, I think, no more pitiful story than that of the last days of the subject of this sketch. Not even the last days of Jonathan Swift exhibit a more painful spectacle than the final scenes in the death-in-life of James Thomson. The craving for stimulants which, ever since he had left the army, had been the bane of his life, and which, whenever a brighter prospect had opened before him, had always destroyed it, had gained a complete dominion over his infirm and broken will, and he was now little better than a derelict, bruised and battered in the battle of life, and drifting helplessly towards the inevitable end.

Even now it is not possible for me to think of the closing scenes of the poet's life without experiencing a new sense of the acute pain which affected me when I was a witness of the terrible bodily weakness and mental impotence to which the poet, the thinker, and the good friend and cheerful companion, was so often reduced by his one great failing. The truth, indeed, and nothing but the truth, should be told on all occasions; but certainly it is not necessary always to tell the *whole* truth. To tell the whole truth, save in the barest outline, about the last days of James Thomson would only give needless pain to the reader, without affording him any compensating advantage.

In the spring of 1882, Thomson paid a last visit to his Leicester friends. This ended in one of his terrible and uncontrollable fits of alcoholic insanity. When the fit had exhausted itself and its victim, leaving him, as it always did, in a state of utter collapse and nervelessness, Thomson returned to London, from whence, on April 22, he addressed the following letter to Mr. J. W. Barrs :—

" Dear Mr. Barrs,—I scarcely know how to write to you after my atrocious and disgusting return for the wonderful hospitality and kindness of yourself and Miss Barrs. I can only say that I was mad. In one fit of frenzy I have not only lost more than I yet know, and half murdered myself (were it not for my debts I sincerely wish it had been wholly), but justly alienated my best and firmest friends, old and new, both in London and Leicester.

As, unfortunately for myself at least, I am left alive, it only remains for me to endeavour my utmost, by hard and persistent struggling, to repay my mere money debts—for my debts of kindness can never be repaid. If I fail—as very probably I shall fail—the failure will but irresistibly prove what I have long thoroughly believed, that for myself and others I am much better dead than alive.

As apologies would be worse than useless, I will conclude by simply expressing my deep gratitude for your astonishing undeserved goodness to myself, and my best wishes for the welfare of you and yours."

Is there any other letter in existence in which the agony and abasement of a fine and noble spirit is expressed with a greater degree of sincerity and pathos? It was the writer's final cry of anguish and despair ; his last expression of the fact that life, indeed, held nothing good for him, and that in death alone could he now hope for deliverance from his evil destiny. As the two murderers rode through Florence with their " murdered man," so, from this time forth, death accompanied Thomson in all his wanderings, delaying for some six weeks to strike the final blow, but, day by day, sapping the poor remains of his strength and vitality, and ever plunging him into deeper depths of mental and physical ruin and degradation.

Perhaps the reader will ask whether something might not even then have been done by Thomson's friends to save him from his approaching doom? I reply that they would gladly have done anything within their power to rescue him from his misery if it had been possible to do it. But there was only one way in which he might possibly have been saved. If he would have entered a home for inebriates, where intoxicants would have been altogether out of his reach, there might have been a glimmer of hope for him : but when this was proposed to him, he would not listen to the sugges-tion. It was, in truth, impossible for his friends to help him ; for, of all helpless creatures, the victim of intemperance is the one whom it is least possible to help. He had, at last, so tired out the long-enduring patience of his London landlord, that he had been turned out of his lodgings—that is, out of the one small room that was at once workroom, living-room, and bed-chamber to him. He now slept in common lodging-houses when he had the few pence that were necessary to purchase a night's lodging : when he had not, his only home was the streets or the police-station. On one occasion he was sentenced to fourteen days' imprisonment, the sentence being inflicted upon him rather in the hope that it would be beneficial to him than as an actual punishment. The time of his imprisonment was spent in hospital ; and so he came out in a better state than he went in ; but he immediately relapsed into his former hopeless condition. The pen of a Zola alone could depict the abject misery into which he had now fallen ; but had I that pen at command, I certainly would not use it. There is so much unavoidable suffering to be endured in the lives of all of us, that the infliction of unnecessary pain, even though only in a cold and unimpassioned relation of facts, will be avoided by all whose sensibilities are keen, or who feel that there is a certain indecency in unveiling the more pitiful aspects of human nature.

Passing, then, over the details of Thomson's last days, we now come to the final catastrophe. On June 1, 1882, Thomson called upon his friend, Philip Bourke Marston, the poet, who was, in a degree second only to himself, also a victim of a malign fate. Marston, being blind, did not at first realise the terrible state of mental and physical prostration into which his friend had fallen. When it did become apparent to him, he, being alone, knew not how to act. Presently his friend, William Sharp, then known as a poet and critic, but now almost forgotten as such, though well enough remembered from the fact that he achieved, under the pseudonym of "Fiona Macleod," a fame which he could never attain under his own proper appellation, fortunately arrived ; and not long afterwards, Mr. Herbert E. Clarke, also a poet of considerable

note.   From the narratives of these two gentlemen,
the following account of the closing scene of
Thomson's life is derived :—

When Mr. Sharp arrived, he found Marston in a
state of much perturbation of mind.   Thomson
had, it seemed, asked permission of him to lie
down upon his host's bed.   When Mr. Sharp went
into the bedroom and spoke to Thomson, the poet
whispered to him that he was dying.   Lighting a
match, Mr. Sharp caught sight of the ghastly
face of the poet resting upon a blood-stained
pillow.   A blood vessel, or blood vessels, had
broken, and the hemorrhage was terrible.   While
the friends were still discussing what was to be
done. Mr. Clarke arrived, and it became possible
to take the measures necessary under the circumstances.   Leaving Mr. Sharp with Thomson,
Marston and his other friend set off to find the
house in Huntley Street, Tottenham Court Road,
where the poet had formerly lodged.   When they
found it, the landlord told them more emphatically
than politely that he would have nothing more to
do with Thomson, who had once tried to burn the
house down.   It thus became clear to them that
Thomson was homeless.   They knew nothing of
his friends, the Wrights, who would doubtless in
this extremity have taken charge of him.   On
their way back to Marston's rooms, they called
upon a doctor and took him with them.   When
the latter saw Thomson, he at once perceived that
there was little or no hope, and he could only
recommend his immediate removal to a hospital.
A cab was called, and Thomson was conveyed in
it to University College Hospital.   When they got
there, it was some time before Thomson could be
attended to, and he had to lie huddled up on a

bench until the house-physician arrived. At last, still unconscious, he was carried into one of the wards.

The next day, when Marston and Sharp went to visit him at the hospital, they found Thomson conscious and collected, though desperately ill. Nevertheless, he was hopeful of a speedy recovery, and when his friends were leaving him, he sat up in bed and expressed his determination to leave the hospital the following Monday, even if he left it in his coffin. This did, in fact, happen. He died on the evening of Saturday, June 3, and his body was removed from the hospital on the ensuing Monday.

On the following Thursday, June 8, the poet's remains were consigned to their final resting-place at Highgate Cemetery, in the grave where, eight years before, his good friend, Austin Holyoake, had been interred. Many friends were present at the funeral, which was conducted without any religious rites. An adaptation of the Secularist Burial Service, originally composed by Austin Holyoake, was read over the poet's remains by his good and steadfast friend, Mr. Theodore Wright, who afterwards delivered a touching and eloquent address to the mourners who were present. And so the curtain fell upon the final scene of the tragedy—a tragedy compared with which the execution of a Charles the First or a Louis the Sixteenth, if we leave out of sight the political significance of those events and regard only the persons, is but an ordinary melodrama, since they, apart from their adventitious trappings, were but poor and commonplace creatures; whereas the poet was one of the finest and rarest spirits that have ever worn the vestments of mortality.

Anything like an adequate critical estimate of Thomson's achievements as poet and prose writer cannot here be attempted. Perhaps I cannot even now look upon his writings with such a degree of detachment as to make me a competent critic of them. If the following remarks prove helpful in any degree to those who have not yet become acquainted with Thomson's writings, they will have effected all that I have aimed at.

If we are interested in Thomson's writings we shall find, when we come to analyse our feelings about them, that it is because we are interested in the author's personality. In other words, he was rather a subjective than an objective writer.* He belonged to the school of Shelley, Coleridge and Rossetti, rather than to that of Scott, Tennyson and Morris. His genius was intensive rather than extensive. He does not often attempt the dramatic presentation of the world outside himself : he prefers rather to study the workings of his own mind than to observe the evolutions of the great drama of humanity. His own thoughts and emotions were almost exclusively the subjects of his writings. Perhaps his works, while gaining in intensity from this cause, lost something in breadth of sympathy and in sanity of outlook upon life. But every author must work according to the law of his own nature ; and it is not given, even to a Shakespeare, to combine incompatible excellences. Thomson would, doubtless, have been happier if he had not been so constantly engaged in analysing

---

* I do not use the term "subjective" because I like it, but only because it is now the custom to employ it. For myself, I should much prefer to use the term "introspective" as opposed to "objective."

and dissecting his own emotions, sensations and
impulses. He did not sufficiently realise the
thought that, since destiny could not in any way
be moved to favour him, it would be wise on his
part to submit, as far as possible, to its decrees.
He did not—or could not—avail himself of the
common method of assuaging or deadening his
sorrows. Most men and women find a way of
escape from their too-insistent griefs or too-
tormenting thoughts in joining in the social life
around them, and so sinking, in a great degree,
their own existence in that of the community. To
escape in this way from themselves is, indeed, the
great object of the lives of most persons, for few
can endure, for any length of time, to be alone
with themseves, or care to indulge in solitary
reflection. That this is the wisest, as well as the
most natural course for the generality of mankind
can hardly be doubted ; and it is this truth that
Walt Whitman most constantly dwells upon.
Though Thomson had much admiration for
Whitman, and was, in his later life, influenced to
some extent by him, no two writers ever differed
more in character and in outlook upon life than
did the authors of " Leaves of Grass " and " The
City of Dreadful Night." The one rejoiced in the
thought of his kinship to the multitude around
him—

" In all people I see myself, none more and not one a
    barleycorn less,
  And the good or bad I say of myself I say of them "—

the other was only too conscious that he had
little in common with " the average sensual man."
Conscious as he was of his intellectual superiority
to those around him, he was unable to free himself
—or at least not till late in life—from the delusion

that he was a sinner who had sinned the un-
pardonable sin. "The Christian conscience," says
a discerning critic, "survived in him to torment
the sceptic." He had in him the blood, tinctured
with fanaticism and intolerance, of long genera-
tions of Scotsmen, who had bequeathed to him
something of their religious fervour, together with
their not less fervent love of the national drink.
His vigorous intellect enabled him to free himself
from the bondage of Calvinistic theology, but its
poison could not be altogether eliminated from his
system. Few of us can hope to be entirely
emancipated from the evil influences of our ancestry
and early education. It is not possible for many
of us to attain the serene and impartial, if somewhat ironic, attitude of Walt Whitman—

> " I do not despise you priests : all time, the world over :
> My faith is the greatest of faiths, and the least of faiths,
> Enclosing worship ancient and modern, and all between
>   ancient and modern."

The unquestioning optimism and equal acceptance
of the good and evil of human existence which
characterised the American poet were impossible
to Thomson. Most of Whitman's writings seem as
if they had been written in sunshine and open air ;
some of Thomson's might have been written within
the walls of a prison, with ink compounded from
his own blood. There is no greater contrast in all
literature than that between the spirit of "Leaves
of Grass" and that of "The City of Dreadful
Night." Yet there is a likeness between them
in at least one point. Both of them express with
absolute truth and sincerity the inmost nature and
deepest convictions of their authors. They are
not works which please the reader because of their
exquisite literary form rather than by their power

of thought or depth of meaning. Neither was the product of a mind at ease, sporting with its own fancies, and solicitous rather about the form than the substance of its creations. Thomson's art, indeed, though it was never, I think, his first consideration, was yet always adequate to his subject, and he seldom or never failed in wedding a fine thought to its fitting expression. I need not say that this was hardly the case with Whitman, whose artlessness too often degenerates into incoherence or mere formlessness.* But, inviting as the subject of the contrast between the two authors and their works is, I must not now be seduced into any further discussion of it.

It was said long ago of Shelley : † "His poetry contains infinite sadness. It is the morbid expression of a soul 'desperate,' to use the beautiful words of Jeremy Taylor, 'by a too quick sense of a constant infelicity.' Like him who had returned from the valley of the dolorous abyss, the reader hears a voice of lamentation 'wailing for the world's wrong' in accents wild and sweet, yet 'incommunicably strange'; but everything to his sight is dark and cloudy when he attempts to penetrate beyond this obscure depth." These words are certainly not wholly true of Shelley, though they may be true of some of his poems. Shelley's chief characteristic was his unconquerable optimism, which all his bitter experience of life could not altogether subdue. I have quoted the passage,

---

* Whether "Leaves of Grass" will ultimately survive as a living force in literature, cannot as yet be safely prophesied ; but it is at least certain that if it fails to do so, it will be because of its formlessness.

† In an article in *Fraser's Magazine*, 1831.

however, because it is true in the main of Thomson,
if not of Shelley. It is, indeed, not wholly true
even of him, for he, no less than Shelley, had his
hours of hope and exaltation, though these came
too seldom and were too short in duration for him
to derive any permanent benefit from them. The
difference between the two poets would seem to be
that, while optimism was the dominant characteristic of Shelley—though he suffered often enough
from melancholy and depression,—the reverse was
the case with Thomson, whose temperamental
melancholy, however it might be relieved by
occasional gleams of happiness, was too firmly
seated in his constitution ever to be overcome.
Even in his earliest long poem, " The Doom of a
City," it is to be seen how firm a grasp the evil
spirit of pessimism * had already laid upon him.
But to speak as if an influence from the outside
had seized upon him is, I think, to mistake the
cause of his unhappiness. " 'Tis in ourselves that
we are thus or thus,"—and Thomson, as we have
seen already, came to perceive—or at any rate to
believe—that he was what he was not from any
external cause or causes, but from his own indi-
vidual nature. He might as well have attempted

---

* I speak here of pessimism as an evil spirit because,
whatever degree of truth there may be in it as a philosophical theory, it is, I think, certain that it must have, on
all but a very few strong and stoical natures, an influence for
evil rather than for good. If the world, indeed, " holds
nothing good for us," it is then useless to work and strive,
since nothing is to be gained by striving. But with pessimist
and optimist alike, I suspect that their philosophical tenets
have but little influence over their daily life and conduct. I
doubt if there has ever been a philosopher who has at all
times, and under all circumstances, squared his conduct in
perfect accordance with his philosophy.

to escape from his own shadow as from the consequences of those inherited qualities of mind and
heart, which were in fact himself. Men are made
what they are chiefly by their innate dispositions,
and only in a very minor degree by the force of
outward circumstances. It is truer to say that our
inner qualities create our surroundings than that
we are ruled by the accidents of our environment.
I am of course aware that this view will not be
universally accepted, for I know that there are good
people who hold that man is the creature of circumstances, and that he can be moulded by
education and training into a pattern of perfect
excellence. In other words, they think that by
suppressing his most distinctively human qualities
he can be converted into a sort of moral and intellectual eunuch, or into such a bloodless mockery
of manliness as Tennyson's King Arthur. Well,
let those who will entertain that belief: doubtless
it pleases them, and it does no harm, I suppose,
to anyone else. But I must be excused myself
from thinking that the best way of dealing with
human beings is to begin by assuming that it is
possible to divest them of their human nature.

Thomson himself called his life " a long defeat " ;
yet was it really that ? As regards himself and his
personal misfortunes, it was certainly a failure ; but
so was that of Robert Burns, who, at the close of
his brief career, might almost have used the same
words. Yet what seemed failure and defeat to
themselves, we can now see was but the necessary
discipline which was to fit them for their allotted
tasks—

> 'Tis pain and passion form the poet's soul,
> Without them he will never reach his goal :
> He must be racked by grief and tried by fire ;
> See just beyond his reach his great desire ;

> View mediocrity the prize attain,
> And seldom till too late the laurel gain :
> Yet what he is his high reward shall be,
> None else may know such ecstasy as he.

Yes ! the poets who, through their own sufferings, learn to understand and to sympathise with the sufferings of humanity at large, and who, by their power of expression, are able to voice the else-inarticulate griefs and repinings of their fellow-mortals, have one great compensation for all the sorrows they have to endure. " The fine madness " of the poet's brain, which is in truth the faculty by which he sees and apprehends things unseen and unapprehended by the multitude, is to him the source of the most exquisite delight, the most ecstatic exaltation, even though it may be also the source of his most poignant pains, his heaviest afflictions. What king or emperor, however great his power, or however wide his dominions, is the peer of a Traherne or a Blake, who, landless and wealthless as he may be, is yet the owner of an infinite realm, the possessor of the only kind of wealth which is indeed " beyond the dreams of avarice " ?